Making Life Happen On A Budget

Veronica G. Burnette

Making Life Happen On A Budget

Ready Writer Publishing

Copyright

All rights reserved and protected under International Copyright Laws. Any contents of this book including its cover may not be reproduced in whole or in part without the express written permission or consent of the author except in the case of brief quotations embodied in news articles, newsletters, and reviews.

Copyright © 2018 Veronica G. Burnette
All Rights Reserved.

Published by:
Ready Writer Publishing
The United States of America

ISBN: 978-0-9743773-8-4

Veronica G. Burnette
www.veronicaburnette.com

Dedication

To my mom who instilled in me ethics and the value of hard work. You kept food on the table and managed a household with five children all while making life happen for us on a budget.

To my son who came along and brought a great deal of pleasure to my life. Your existence was the extra incentive that helped me endure through my struggles. You caused me to work harder, appreciate the value of money and spend it more wisely.

To all of you who are striving to make ends meet and live life to the fullest. I dedicate this to you and your success.

Acknowledgments

I acknowledge that I did not always have it together. I acknowledge that life and being a single mom striving to make ends meet taught me much wisdom. I acknowledge that without the help of God, family, and friends, I would not be where I am today. I acknowledge that I still do not have all the answers, but what I have learned along the way is valuable. Therefore, I would like to acknowledge anyone and everyone for the help and encouragement to never give up. Although there are too many to mention by name, I thank you for patiently sticking with me and by me through the rough times.

Contents

Introduction 11

Saving On a Budget 17

Shopping on a Budget............................. 27

Cooking & Eating on a Budget 41

Traveling On A Budget 49

Getting Married on a Budget 69

Purchasing a Home on a Budget................ 81

Car Purchase on a Budget 99

Furnishing on a Budget 109

Teaching Children to Budget................... 119

At the End of the Day............................. 129

About the Author 133

*Wisdom is the principal thing; therefore get wisdom: and with all thy getting get understanding.
(Proverbs 4:7)*

Introduction

There used to be a television show called "The Lifestyles of the Rich and Famous" that aired from 1984 to 1995. It featured the lives of wealthy millionaires and billionaires. Who among us considered to be "working class" citizens have ever fantasized about being delivered from the habit of having to report to work for a living? If you are among those who are rich and famous, this book is not for you. My focus is on those who, like me, understand the struggles and the juggling of money to make ends meet. I do believe there are many.

A feast is made for laughter, and wine maketh merry: but money answereth all things (Ecclesiastes 10:19)

It is often said, "money can't buy happiness." I agree that it may not be able to purchase happiness, but in many ways, it makes life easier. It is the answer to many problems. Ask those who get up every morning and go to work. They are not going because they want to, but because they must work to live and be comfortable. It is the "American Dream" to own a home, have nice cars, raise a family and have a few luxuries along the way. These things do not simply fall out of the sky, nor have I have seen "Publishers Clearing House" knock on any doors in my neighborhood with any winning checks.

If my life were to be an open book, I would want it to read like a self-help tutorial. Life is not always about learning what to do, but it is also learning from the mistakes. We may often appear to others to have it all together, but that is usually not the case. There is a story that each of us is living behind closed doors. Behind those doors is where we endure the true test of faith.

Making ends meet is often one of those struggles.

Experiencing setbacks, having to raise a child as a single parent and the absence of a second household income was no easy feat. This is where my spending habits took a drastic turn. There were days I was so broke I could barely pay attention.

I was forced to learn how to manage money in ways I had not considered before. To be honest, the need to manage had not always been important because there was always extra to put aside for a rainy day. Unfortunately, my rainy day appeared when divorce hit my life.

My credit score went from excellent to almost being nonexistent. The fact was that no one would consider giving me a credit card or a loan based on my credit score. This was both disappointing and heartbreaking. It also caused me to feel like a failure. Looking back on things, I now recognize there were moments I could have made better decisions. Nonetheless, because I could not change the past, I became focused on repairing the damage. Wisdom has taught me to learn from my mistakes. It is not enough to simply go on. We must learn to **grow** on instead.

If I had only known then what I know now, my bank account would be sending me thank-you letters. I have found there is an art to spending money. If you are willing to work the system, the system will work for you. I don't know too many people who have dollar bills lying around waiting to be thrown away like yesterday's trash.

You would not think those who are rich would have to worry about a budget. It may not be like the budget sheet of the working class. I believe those who fall into the "rich" category have a budget plan as well. Otherwise, those who are rich would not continue to stay that way. The simple truth is, a budget is nothing more than a plan of action. It is the process of understanding what you have in order to calculate and maneuver in the direction toward obtaining the desired results.

I used to believe that if I could only hit the lottery, my life would be wonderful. Don't get me wrong, winning the lottery can benefit one greatly. However, I have since learned that my life is already wonderful. Maturity has afforded me the ability to see it through a different set of lenses. Knowing what I know now, even if I were to win the lottery, I would still stick to a plan of action called a budget. Why? I believe no matter how much money you have, spending it haphazardly, in my opinion, is not being a wise manager. Take a look at the many who have won the lottery only to lose it all and end up bankrupt later.

There are avenues and ways to budget from very simple to complex. I have not gathered an all-inclusive list of ways to save money. Herein are just a few helpful tips and tools I have found useful in my life as a working adult.

There are countless programs to teach individuals how to budget time and money. However, the focus of this little how-to book is to provide you with a few tips.

These simple, but informative tips are things I have learned through trial and error, mistakes, and conquests of money matters.

Wisdom is the principal thing; therefore get wisdom: and in all thy getting get understanding. (Proverbs 4:7)

There is a saying "what you don't know won't hurt you," but I beg to differ. What you don't know will cost you, by causing you to spend unnecessarily. Learning comes through experience. I love sharing my knowledge, experiences, tips, and tools with family and friends. Now I am sharing this information with the hope that you will use it to have more successes than errors. Your life matters, so let's make it count. Let's budget our way towards turning those dreams into reality.

Chapter 1

Saving On a Budget

I was not born eating from a gold-plated spoon. I watched my mother raise five children and manage to make ends meet. She is a strong woman who taught all of her children the value of hard work. My father died when I was six years old, and my mother was left to raise five children on her own. Taking care of a household of six is rarely easy without an income from both parents. Imagine trying to make life happen with limited funds. Nonetheless, she managed and managed well. I can't recall ever having to be without the necessities. My mother was quite resourceful and always made a way.

In the midst of it all, I watched her add what little she could to a savings account. Once upon a time, as part of the school curriculum, we were taught simple banking techniques such as opening accounts and writing checks. Long gone are those days. Nonetheless, by the time I got to this point in school I was already equipped because my mom taught us the process. She would allow us to write the checks to pay the bills. Little did I know, this was part of her lessons on how to manage a household and be self-sufficient. A few of the things I admire are her determination, work ethics and "make it happen" attitude. By watching her, I've learned much about survival.

Tip #1

"A Little Goes A Long Way"

A penny saved is a penny earned. Once upon a time you would see a penny lying on the ground and pick it up. Now, most of the time, we see pennies lying around and continue walking over them. I believe this is because the value of a penny has diminished. There is not much you can buy with a penny, but pennies still make dollars. So, let's not discount the penny.

In the same way, we should not discount minor deductions. A small deduction from your paycheck each week can add up. After a while, you will not notice. What you will notice, however, is the increase in your savings account each month.

Gathering with family and friends during the holiday season is quite memorable. We all enjoy seeing our children's eyes light up when they are opening their presents. It's all a part of making life happen. Some banks have what they call a "Christmas Club" whereby you establish an amount of funds to be deducted from your pay until a set calendar date. The idea is so that you will have the necessary funds to spend during the holiday season. If you can save for Christmas, why not continue those savings on a continual basis?

There are other ways to invest and put money aside such as IRAs, CDs, mutual fund, stocks, bonds and the like. Whatever type of account you deem necessary that best meets both your short and long-term goals, the purpose is to save money.

We invest our time and energy in many things. Why not invest in your future and the future of your children whenever possible. Take a look at this simple formula. $14 per week adds up to $728 per year. That amounts to $2 per day. Over the course of 5 years, you will have saved $3,640. If you decide to double that amount you will have saved $7,280 at the end of five years. The amount does not include interest. When possible, increase the amount of money you are putting aside. Your account will thank you for it.

Another simple tip is to take all of your loose change at the end of the day, week, or month and put it in a jar. At the end of the year, count it. You will be surprised at how much you have collected. This approach can be used to help your children learn how to save and invest money as well.

Saving might not be the priority when looking at the amount of the debt you have or the bills you are having to pay. However, in the grand scheme of things, we often spend more on coffee and soda pop. That probably adds up to at least two or three dollars per a day.

Despite what you may believe, a little does go a long way. It may take some time to build, but it will grow if you let it. If you are not already doing something like this, there is no time like the present. It only takes a few minutes to meet with a bank representative to acquire the necessary information to make an informed decision about all your monetary investments.

Tip #2

"The Envelope System"

A little budgeting tip I learned some years ago is called the "envelope system." It is the process of getting a set of envelopes and putting enough cash in each to cover the cost of your monthly bills and the little extra excursions that require money. The extra would be a night out with friends, hair, nails, etc. Once you have spent all that is in a particular envelope, you have exhausted your spending in that category for the month. You are not allowed to "rob Peter to pay Paul." In other words, you must refrain from touching anything in the other envelopes even if there was extra left over from those categories. Any extra funds can be set aside in a rainy day account or a simple savings account.

When committed, this can be an excellent way to keep from overspending. It will require a degree of discipline that will pay off in the end.

Tip #3

"Over Draft"

Once upon a time, mankind would write checks to pay for things. The beautiful thing about writing a check was that it took a few days before it reached the bank to be deducted from your account. At that time, retailers and financial institutions used snail mail to process paperwork. I took advantage of the processing system.

My paydays for the most the part, have always been on Fridays. When I knew a payday was approaching, I would write a check a couple of days before payday in order to purchase what I needed. I knew my paycheck would be deposited into my account before the check I had written would get there. This was a little risky, but when the demands outweigh the supply, you take a few risks.

To give you an idea of what I mean. At one point in time, I had no money to cover the cost of an emergency. Desperate times called for desperate measures. I found myself having to write a $2.00 check. Yes, you read that right. The check was for $2.00, and my account had $0 funds.

The transaction fee on my checking account at that time for "insufficient funds" was $35.00. Therefore, I found myself having to chase that $2.00 check to the bank. If the store had cashed the check before I had a chance to make a deposit, that little $2.00 check would have cost me $37.00. Yes, the struggle was indeed real.

There are still a few who use checks, but not too many since the invention of debit cards. Even when using a check, the funds are immediately deducted from the account because retailers are now using scanners. Once the check is scanned, they will return it to you because they no longer have to mail it to the bank. If the funds are not there, your transaction will be declined, and in some cases, a transaction fee applied.

Things happen, and one insufficient funds fee can have a catastrophic effect on a checking account. That is why it is important to have overdraft protection plan in place.

Modern technology has afforded us the opportunity to function without cash or checks on hand since being introduced to the debit card and automatic draft. Having debit cards is the same thing as having cash. Using a debit card in some cases is helpful because it causes us to exercise a little more discipline. If there are no funds in your account, that means there is no money to spend.

Have you ever suffered the embarrassment of hearing "your transaction was declined?" I know this has hurt my ego on a few occasions. This is what I meant when I said debit cards can help us exercise discipline. Notice I said **DEBIT** card, not credit card. There is a difference.

There is a system the banks use called overdraft protection. Using this can create another problem, however, within in your budget plan if and when it is not used wisely. Keep in mind this is your savings account and not some pot of funds to be used as cash on hand. Fight it! It's only an illusion. Overdraft protection should only be used as an emergency back up and not a go-to solution when you want to splurge. It depletes and defeats the purpose of saving. Besides, there are fees attached to using overdraft protection. This is an unnecessary waste of funds that add up over time.

Depending on the banking institution, their system will allow a certain number of overdraft transactions within a month or a certain period before a transaction fee is charged and deducted from your account. Here again, ask questions, do your research, and read the fine print before you sign up.

Chapter 2

Shopping on a Budget

It is always a good day to shop. I have found that you can be trendy without spending your entire paycheck. I don't know about you, but wherever I can save a dollar, I'm on it. I would rather spend my money doing something I love like biking and traveling, for example. Traveling on a budget is another area we will discuss in this little book of tips.

Buying on sale allows me to save money and put those extra dollars toward other extracurricular activities. I believe in looking and feeling good wherever I am in the world. If you budget properly, you will also be able to do many things you desire without starving your bank account.

Like many of us, I get excited when I find a beautiful outfit for sale. This is especially true when I see the price tag of what it once cost at the original retail price. Let's be honest. It feels good sometimes to get a lot for a little. It is often assumed by my co-workers and friends that I pay a lot of money for my attire. They are often quite surprised when I inform them of the opposite. When I share with them what I am sharing with you, they get excited.

I have shopped in some of the major department stores and purchased entire ensembles for under $40. You may be thinking "they must be the cheap no-name items." On the contrary, these items are in fact name brand. Maybe they are not the top of the line, but they are name brand items nonetheless. I am not out to impress the world with how much money I can afford to spend. Spending a lot of money can be quite challenging on the average working-class salary. However, if spending appeals to your taste, that's fine. If you can afford to spend and maintain a comfortable lifestyle, I encourage you to do whatever you need to do to make your life happen. My budget has not always afforded me the comfort of making high-end purchases. Although I am better able to do so now, I still would rather purchase on sale. Besides, I would rather spend my money on traveling. My current focus is on experiencing the world and all of its beauty.

My shopping tips are often incorporated and used by many, while others reject my ideas and ways of saving money. How unfortunate, because many of us work hard for our money. I am sure we can agree that it helps to save when and where we can.

Tip #1

"Wait For It"

When an item first hits the scene, it may have the "WOW, I just have to have it" effect. I guarantee the items you are dreamy-eyed about will eventually go on sale.

I saw a beautiful blouse on the home shopping network (HSN). The cost was $69.00, but over the next three weeks, the price dropped to $9.99. Then I waited until that one day of the week they offer free shipping. It was at that moment I decided to make the purchase. Notice the price difference. It will take patience and discipline but give waiting a try.

What if they sell out of my size or color? This is something to consider as you will be taking a risk especially if it is an exclusive item or designer item such as you would find on the home shopping networks. In this case, you may have to bite the bullet and pay the extra if it really a must have. Here is one of those situations when you need to ask yourself the hard shopper's question, "Do I really need that?" or "Is it worth the money I'm about to spend?"

If this is a major retailer and they run out of what you want at one store, there is good news. In many cases, the item(s) can be found in another store or in their warehouse. Instead of wasting gas driving around to pick up your item(s), ask if delivery is available. If you find that delivery is available to your home, make sure to ask about free shipping. They may not offer if you do not ask. If you discover there is a fee for shipping, ask if they would be willing to waive the charge. Because they want to move the inventory, they may be happy to accommodate.

Shipping is also an option to consider when traveling. I have shopped in many stores across the United States. Because the airlines are so finicky about luggage weight, I will make my purchases, and have my items shipped home for little to no shipping cost.

Tip #2

"Coupons are Money Savers"

If you can help it, NEVER shop without coupons. If you do not have a coupon, there are countless mobile apps you can download on your mobile devices to use for saving. Retail-Me-Not, Ebates, and Groupon are just to name a few. Make sure to stay up to date as mobile apps are being created and made available quite regularly these days. Major retail chains have mobile apps that give you access to their coupons and special offers.

A good sale can be quite enticing. It is described by shopaholics as a euphoric adrenaline rush. Retailers are counting on us to take the bait. Retailers buy in bulk, which means the purchased items have been mass produced. What they do not tell you is their markup is more than 100%. That is why the retailer can afford to sell these items at such a discounted rate and still make money. Most of the time when you see the word "sale," it really isn't a sale at all. It is a marketing ploy designed to entice you into thinking you're saving money. They simply mark up the price to make it appear they are placing the item on sale.

Another way to use your coupon is to split your purchases into chunks. If you have a coupon that is $10 off of $25, this means you only have to spend $25 to use that particular coupon. If you are purchasing more than one item, you can split the purchase up and use the coupon more than once saving $10 on each purchase. Many retailers have no restrictions on how many times they will allow you to use a coupon. However, there are some that will keep your coupon once you use it. Just remember to read the fine print.

Tip #3

"Will That Be Cash or Credit"

Cash is always a good option versus using a credit card. This alleviates the threat of identity theft, fraud, etc. I do recommend having one or two major credit cards for emergencies or other necessary things that require the use of one. I would suggest doing your research to determine the cost of interest, annual dues, and membership fees before you apply for the card.

There is a Capital One commercial, most of which is featuring Samuel L. Jackson. At the end of the commercial, he asks the question, "What's in your wallet?" Every merchant wants you to have their name in your wallet. I am not a fan of credit cards primarily because of the high-interest rates attached to them. However, one way to own credit cards and avoid paying interest is to pay off the amount of your purchase immediately. There is no penalty with many creditors for paying off your balance early. That means you will still obtain your points and other perks associated with your purchases.

Using a store credit card is an excellent way to acquire additional coupons, assuming you want to go through the hassle of applying and owning one. Again, I would caution you to check the fine print. You will be surprised by what is overlooked. You will most definitely want to check the interest rates before you give your consent.

Depending on the amount of money you spend, you can accumulate coupons. To get an additional percentage off of your purchase, the retailer may require you to make the purchase using your card. If you do not have their credit card, the extra savings is a marketing strategy that entices many into applying for one. Keep in mind that interest will begin to accrue on those purchases if the balance is not paid in full by the end of the billing cycle. If you do not have the funds to pay the balance, not using the card at all is a good rule to follow. In other words, use the card for the perks, but make sure to maintain a $0 balance.

Tip #4

"Buy Off Season"

One thing is for sure, as long as the earth remains, there will be winter, spring, summer, fall, and Christmas. It comes the same time every year. How many times have you said to yourself "I wish I had purchased that when it was on sale?"

We know that at the end of the season just about everything goes on sale. This is the time to really make your dollars work for you. Retailers are banking on your bucks, especially during the holiday season. It is reported by all major news networks that "Black Friday" and "Cyber Monday" are two of the most profitable days for retailers. They already know these are the days shoppers spend the most money. This is a time when sales are in abundance. Because new items are on their way in, they will want to move current and any of last year's inventory. Couple this with tip #2 about using coupons. You will be able to walk away with some steals and deals.

This is where your coupon apps along with any accessible store coupons will come in handy as well. When the item is already 50% off, and you have an additional coupon worth 25% off, you will walk away feeling accomplished.

Here is an idea if you are one who loves to give gifts. This is a smart and economical way to buy gifts on a budget. Why not shop for next year's Christmas gifts during this year's sale? This is especially true for those of us who have children. That is what many consumers do on Black Friday. We not only buy gifts, but decorations, household goods, and other items you need. I was a working-class single mom on a budget. This was the strategy I used 90% of the time when making purchases for my son and our household.

Tip #5

"Hold Onto Your Receipts"

Many retailers nowadays have a 90-day or more return policy. Therefore, it is a good idea to hold on to your receipts. Some will allow you to return the item no matter how long ago you made the purchase.

If an item goes on sale after you have purchased it, some retailers will allow you to return it for the lesser price. That's if the item has not been used or worn of course. Although some will even allow the return after you've used the item **IF** it is simply not working for you. In exchange, however, their policy may only allow you to receive store credit in this case. You will probably be more successful in receiving monetary refunds with the larger retail merchants; your mom & pop stores, not so much. They can't afford to take the loss. This does not apply to all. Every store is governed by its own set of rules. Therefore, always read the fine print and double check with the store on their return policy to avoid any surprises.

Tip #6

"Price Matching"

"If you find it at a lower price, we will match it and give you an additional 10% off." Does this sound familiar? This is a marketing strategy retailers use to earn your money. When possible, take advantage of their offer by using your smartphone apps to find lower prices.

Because competition is fierce among retailers these days, most stores will price match or give you an additional percentage lower than what their competitor is offering. Ask about their "price match" policy as they vary based on the retailer. Everyone is not considered a competitor. Do not assume a given retailer will price match against everyone. Save time by asking what stores they price match against. Many will honor and match major competitors such as Amazon, Walmart, Target, etc.

Believe or not, some retailers' online prices are often different from the prices you see in the store. In this case, the retailer will most often honor their online price. Take a few moments to do an online check, especially for items that have significant price tags. This also applies to other stores within their chain. When you find a lower price in one of the merchant's other stores within the area, ask if they will honor the lower price. Never pay more if you can avoid it.

Chapter 3

Cooking & Eating on a Budget

Reflecting on what my mother taught me growing up, I realize she was a budget professional. Most children look forward to the last day of school. However, when I was younger, I hated it. What could be so bad about the last day of school? I'm glad you asked. I spent my summers helping my mom prepare for the winter. This meant weeks of cleaning, picking, canning and freezing vegetables from the garden. What child wants to do that? I sure didn't. I vowed that once I became grown, I would never do it again. Well, guess what? I now look forward to the summer months so I can put away fresh vegetables.

I did not understand the value of the lessons my mother was instilling in me at the time. I can say without hesitation that I am truly grateful for those lessons. Not only do I have fresh vegetables all year long, I also have the benefit of eating healthy in the process.

There is always time for soup. My mother made some of the best soups with ingredients left over during the week. To this day whenever I make a pot of soup, I will add kielbasa sausage. My mother used hot dogs. With kids, some food is simply not appealing. I believe the hot dogs are what made the soup more appealing. I have noticed over the years this has become a staple ingredient. All of my sisters and brother add some form of sausage or hot dog to their soups.

Working a full-time job and finding time to prepare a good meal every day is just another something added to an already busy schedule. Picking up something quick and eating out may be convenient, but it can also become expensive and wreak havoc on a budget.

Everyone deserves a meal out with friends or sometimes alone every now and again. When it comes to sticking to a budget, it is important to weigh your options and consider the long-term costs.

During Michelle Obama's time as FLOTUS, she brought great attention to eating healthy. It is possible to find really inexpensive fast food meals. The question is, are they healthy and are they good for you? One way of answering that question and know for sure is to prepare meals for yourself. Put the art of cooking back in the kitchen. There are tons of flavor-filled, inexpensive, quick and healthy meal options available. It will require not only budgeting but time management as well.

Tip #1

"Couponing"

I'm sure this goes without saying, but coupons can be your best friend when it comes to eating out and buying food and groceries. You may have heard of the television show called "Extreme Couponing" where individuals use their coupon-clipping skills as a sport. Instead of paying for groceries, I have seen episodes where the buyer receives a refund from the amount of coupons used. This indeed takes time and attention. It has become a full-time job for some. I guess that is why they call it "extreme."

We discussed using coupon apps in the previous chapter. This is another place those apps are very beneficial. Paper coupon versions are still available but can be a little cumbersome at times. With the mobile version, you lose the need to keep up with so many. It is, of course, a personal preference. Pay attention to store policy as many will honor their competitor's coupons to win your business.

Don't be quick to give up. It will take consistency to reap the benefits. On the bottom of most receipts, it shows how much you saved when buying on sale or using coupons. As an extra incentive when possible, set aside the amount you are saving and watch it accumulate. This will be a huge boost to your confidence that you are indeed making a difference in your budget.

Tip #2

"Cooking Versus Eating Out"

For all those early morning risers who enjoy getting up early and preparing for the day; kudos and hats off to you. For those who turn off the alarm clock for another extra five-minute snooze, then another and another, I am starting a support group for us. If I do not prepare my lunch the night before, more than likely, I will not take time to do it before I walk out the door. This means having to purchase lunch or eating something unhealthy. This can be quite costly. That five dollar lunch multiplied by five days a week equals $25.00. When multiplied by four, that becomes $100 per month. That equates to a household bill or possibly two.

What used to be called leftovers, is now more eloquently referred to as "meal prepping." Food savers are good when it comes to preparing meals and preserving food, especially when buying in bulk. In a household of two, buying in bulk can save you money when these items are preserved properly. It saves you from having to run back and forth to the store every week. This not only saves time, but it also saves money on the cost of fuel. Let's face it, with the fluctuation in gasoline prices, this can be an extra expense avoided.

Eating out at a nice restaurant does not have to be expensive. You just have to know how and where to look. Search for restaurant coupons such as Groupon, Ebates, and Zoot, to name a few. There are countless others. If you do not find something suitable to your taste buds on a budget, keep looking. Some restaurants may offer unadvertised specials for the eat-in customers only.

Tip #3

"Meal Pooling"

We have heard of carpooling. It is an arrangement among a group of automobile owners where each driver transports the others or their children to and from a designated place. Why not try meal-pooling? What is meal-pooling? I'm glad you've asked. It is the same concept as carpooling, except you and a group of trusted friends share the responsibility of preparing meals. It takes the pressure off of having to prepare meals every day or every week.

The object is for each friend to take turns cooking the meal(s) as agreed upon by the group. Imagine the extra time to do other things as well as being able to enjoy a home-cooked meal.

Make couponing and shopping a group activity. You could even have a joint account to deposit and pull from as agreed upon by the group as well. This could be a fun, team/friend building experience.

Chapter 4

Traveling On A Budget

For many who fall into the "working class" category, we often find ourselves having to decide whether to pay a bill or sacrifice and take a well-deserved vacation. As a single mom, this was my constant struggle. Each time, paying the bill would win the vote. There is a saying "hindsight is 20/20." This is very true. As I look back, I can see how with a little ingenuity, I could have done both. It may have taken a little longer, but it could have been done. Other than the theme park visits and local beach trips here and there, it was 20 years before I had a real travel experience. I promised myself that once I had reached a certain point in life, I would take my son on the trip of a lifetime. I figured lifetime adventures would cost a pretty penny. To my surprise, I discovered that a beautiful adventure can be quite affordable.

One of the biggest events I wanted to celebrate was my son's graduation from college. I felt he deserved it after such an accomplishment. Besides, I had never really taken him anywhere. I felt I owed it to him and myself. Since I love being a part of first-time memories, I wanted it to be a trip that he would remember because it was one of his first. "I know, he has never been on a cruise. This is something we can do together" I thought. I had been on a cruise before but did not have to bother with the travel arrangements. I was given the cost and told what and how to pay. This time, it would be different. It was during my research that I discovered a few things.

I have traveled internationally a few times and have since learned it is not as expensive as I once thought. Somewhere in my head, I saw high dollar signs and impossibilities. That is the furthest thing from the truth. Traveling can be as glorious and expensive as one is willing to pay. I'm sure that many of us would love to have the luxury of owning a private jet like the one Richard Gere used to carry Julia Roberts to a night out at the ballet in the movie "Pretty Woman." Unfortunately, that is not a reality for those who struggle to make ends meet working an everyday nine-to-five. Nonetheless, I have learned that traveling does not have to be as expensive as I once believed.

Getting caught up in the excitement of getting away can be overwhelming. I encourage you to take time and do your research. It can save you a few dollars, which can be used as spending money when you get to your destination.

Speaking of spending money, this is something that should be budgeted as well. If it is not properly budgeted, it can quickly lead to overspending. You get to your island oasis and get caught up in the nostalgia of island beauty. You whip out your credit card and make those unplanned purchases. Ask yourself, "Do I really need what I am about to purchase?" Keep in mind that the bill you are making will have to be paid when you get back home. It is perfectly normal to purchase some memorabilia from your trip. Just don't get carried away and bring home a bunch of unnecessary trinkets that become nothing more than dust collectors to be sold at the next yard sale.

Souvenirs are great in the fact that they allow others to enjoy the experience of your travel. However, they also cost money. Besides, how many of your family and friends appreciate, display or even use the souvenirs you buy them? Gift shop prices can be quite expensive. The markups for their merchandise is most incredible. So, when making these purchases, consider the cost, the room it will take up in your luggage, and whether it be a waste of precious dollars you could use for something else.

It is okay to dream, but we have to be real and honest with ourselves. Traveling can become an expensive habit. A budget will help you stay focused. Adhering to the plan will keep you from drifting into that faraway place of make-believe where expense is not a concern.

I often travel and continue to look for places and ways to travel worldwide. Because I now know the possibilities of worldwide travel can be accomplished through thoughtful consideration and careful planning, I look forward to every opportunity to explore and encounter the new and different throughout my journeys within this beautiful place called earth.

Plot your destination, map your plans, and save your money. There is no time like the present. Let's plan a trip.

Tip #1

"Choose Your Destination"

Where are some of the places you would like to visit? Is this destination a long-term or short-term goal? The answer to this question will be the amount of money it will take to get there. Don't fret, as there are many places to go between now and reaching your long-term goal destinations. If you budget right, you can save for both simultaneously.

Once you have decided on your destination, will you travel by car, boat, train or plane? If you are like me, I prefer the destination more than traveling to get there, although that can be an adventure in itself.

Tip #2

"Mode of Operandi"

In the words of Dr. Seuss from the book Green Eggs and Ham; "I could not, would not, on a boat. I will not, will not, with a goat. I will not eat them in the rain. I will not eat them on a train." Daniel was protesting his dislike for green eggs and ham. It sounds like some of us when it comes to our mode of travel. There are those who are very much against flying. Some are even afraid of getting on a boat. Such fears are going to make traveling a challenge for you. One good thing is that it will help you save on your budget. However, if you are one of those with the "wanderlust" gene, exploring the world is the only cure.

In some cases flying international can be quite expensive, but this is not always the case. There is good news, flying can be affordable. You might be thinking, "No Way!" The answer is "Yes, Way." Depending on the airline you choose, you can obtain some great deals. This may be determined by the time of year you are traveling and how far in advance you book your flight. Sometimes you may find a last-minute deal. They fall under what some airlines and travel companies label as "last minute getaways." This does not leave much room for planning. If you are one of those spontaneous personalities, this will work well for you.

Airfare mobile apps can be quite useful when comparing prices. There are quite a few at your disposal. You can also program them to alert you when prices update. When those prices drop, you are alerted immediately. Using the same app, you can then make your purchase if the price agrees with your budget.

If you like being on the open waters, cruising is the way to go. Getting the window view or balcony suite would be ideal. However, those will cost a bit more than the interior cabins. Given the amount of activity on a cruise ship, it is highly unlikely you will be spending much time in your room. So, is the price of a balcony all that important? If you like your privacy and spending quiet time in your room, then a balcony may be the way to go. It is a good way to be in a crowd and yet be isolated all at the same time. You simply weigh your options and determine what is more important and best for you based on how much you are willing to spend.

A huge benefit to cruising is there is no need to budget for lodging or meals because they are all included. My son and I traveled to Bermuda on a seven-day adventure. The only cost other than the cruise itself was the expense of excursions. Since we had on board credits, we took advantage and did a little scuba diving. The price difference between the balcony, the ocean view, and the interior was quite different. I opted for the interior since it was one-third of the cost of the balcony and cheaper than the interior cabin. For a seven day trip, the cost was $1,500 for two.

If you do decide to book an interior suite, never hesitate to ask for a free upgrade. If there are rooms available, most cruise lines will work with you. Since they are a customer service driven industry, they are often willing to accommodate. A huge part of their advertisement is word of mouth. What is the likelihood that you will book with them again if your experience was anything less than exceptional? Besides, what is the worst that can happen? They just might say "Yes."

Check with the country or destination you plan to visit to determine their peak season. Then make your plans during off-peak seasons. This could cut your costs tremendously.

Tip #3

"A Bundle of Joy"

Can we say "all-inclusive?" When traveling abroad, you might want to consider going with the all-inclusive package. This option usually includes airfare. As with the cruise ship experience, everything you need is taken care of all in one place. Unlike the cruise ship, a big difference is that your alcohol is included if you are a drinker. You never have to leave the resort. But of course, you will because there is so much to see and do. You can go at it alone and piecemeal your package. But why do that, when there are a ton of travel sites that have already done the work.

No need to use a travel agent unless you just want to spend extra money to have someone do the work for you. By cutting out the middleman, you will be saving some dough. Tons of travel sites are user-friendly. Some require total payment at the time of booking, but others will allow you to make payments over time. This is not a bad option. However, you will want to check the fine print. These days, many of the major airlines have their trip advisors. You can book your vacation package through them as well. I have found that when you bundle, you receive more discounts. Make sure to check the fine print and ask about the refund policy. As with any company, they are in the business of making money, and there are many criteria.

Travel insurance is something else to consider. Having it is not mandatory, but I highly recommend making the purchase. It is an added expense, but well worth the peace of mind. Some health insurance plans within the United States do not provide coverage when traveling abroad, but your travel insurance does. It will refund your money in full or in part depending on the type of insurance you purchase. Another option that insurance provides is credit toward another trip if something happens and you are not able to travel. Check out your options and remember to ask all the right questions.

Tip #4

"Vehicle Rental"

Renting a car may be a little tricky. This may require some additional phone calls or surfing the internet to find deals. When this option is available, you can take advantage of something I discovered called the "mystery car" deal. This is where a rental car company has an abundance of a certain type of vehicle in their inventory that did not rent that day. In order to keep inventory moving, the company is willing to rent the car at an extremely cheap rate. You will not know what type of car it is until you go to retrieve it. Depending on how generous the agent is feeling that day, s/he may be nice and tell you beforehand what type of vehicle you will be renting.

It is a simple process. You can do this by visiting any travel website that has multiple listings and price comparisons such as Travelocity, Expedia, etc. Choose your dates. Scroll down through the available vehicles. You will see a car that has a car cover over it. That is the mystery car. The good news is you are not obligated as they do not require you to enter any credit card information. Therefore, if you get to the pickup site and decide you do not want that type of vehicle, oh well. You have the option of renting something else or simply walking away. Easy-breezy, right? This is the current state of affairs. Things could change at any time. So take advantage of it while you can.

Another good thing about this process is there are no predetermined time constraints on booking beforehand. You could be standing in the rental car agency and still go through the process to secure this vehicle. How cool is that?

Tip #5

"Price Matching"

Here is another opportunity for a bidding war. Price matching seems to be the name of the game these days. When booking components of your trip, check to see if the company you are using will price match to win your business. Most will if the company they are being asked to price match has the same itinerary you are attempting to book. If they are not willing, by all means, go with another company who will.

Pay close attention before you agree. What some consumers may not know is that some of the travel companies appear to be different when in fact, they are the same. They list themselves as individual entities, but they are a part of the same parent company. This is one reason they are so willing to price match what you find with one of their sister companies.

There are many companies willing to accept your money and provide you with a few perks for booking with them. If you are traveling in a group, there will be extra perks involved if you are acting as the agent. This will be discussed in the next travel tip. Remember, they will not tell you if you do not ask. Therefore, make sure you ask.

Tip #6

"Just a Moment of Your Time"

Attending a timeshare presentation for a free vacation is another excellent way to travel on a budget. Timeshares are arrangements whereby people own the right to use a shared property for a designated period of time. This is usually one or two weeks out of the year.

To get this "free" vacation, you will be required to attend a sales presentation which can last anywhere from one hour to one day. Before you sign on the dotted line, make sure you have a clear understanding of how long the presentation is going to be. Then ask yourself how much time you are willing to invest. When the timeline is agreeable, go for it. What is a little time out of your day, given the fact that the rest of the time is yours to spend however you want on their dime.

The presentation can be quite alluring. Stay focused! Stay strong! Even if you have every intention of saying no, every part of the sales pitch is carefully designed to convince you it is too good a deal to pass up. Do not allow yourself to get caught up in the hype. The salesperson is counting on your vulnerability.

One drawback is that you will have to provide your own transportation. Not to worry even if it is too far to drive. There are plenty of airfare deals, even on international trips.

Tip #7

"You Be the Agent"

When booking a group traveling event, ask the company you're booking with for freebies. You can also negotiate in a way that your travel will cost you nothing. This is how many trip planners travel so extensively. They almost never pay. The fact that they have successfully booked a group trip affords them the pleasure of traveling for free. For example, you decide to book a vacation for a group of 50 people. The fact that you are acting as your own travel agent and booking through their company, free accommodations for booking with them may be offered to you.

You can involve yourself as little or as extensively as you wish. It all depends on the amount of work you are willing to put into setting up a group itinerary. It will require a significant amount of patience to deal with people's tendency toward indecision. Will you be the one to establish and plan group participation and activities?

You get to decide. Keep in mind, the more details you include, the more you will have to deal with people and their indecisiveness. Keep it simple and let the group plan their own events and excursions.

Does this obligate you to stay with the group? Absolutely not! Once you all reach your destination, you are on your own to do whatever you wish with your time. It's all up to you. You are simply the point person who put the plan into action; thereby you are benefiting from all of your hard work.

Never be afraid to ask for upgrades. Many times if the cruise line, flight, resort or hotel is not completely booked at the time of your trip, they may be willing to allow free upgrades to first class, a balcony versus a window view, or an oceanfront suite upon your arrival and per your request.

This is an excellent tip for all types of travel. The key is to ask questions and do your research. It may be a little time consuming, but the benefits are well worth the effort.

Chapter 5

Getting Married on a Budget

Most of us dream of that fairytale wedding and gala affair. It is not every day that we get to marry the love of our lives. But when we do, we want to celebrate this joyous occasion with our family and friends. We tend to go all out to make this occasion as special and memorable as possible. However, memories can be quite expensive.

The wedding is an area where many go overboard with the spending. We get caught up in the excitement of the occasion and can't see past the diamonds in our eyes.

Event planning is an entrepreneurial career path many are choosing to take. The income from this career is quite lucrative. Weddings are a part of this booming industry. If you don't think so, look at the number of network shows geared toward marriage and the extravagance of it all. There is one show called "Say Yes to the Dress" that displays some of the world's most famous designer dresses along with their hefty price tags.

We have become hypnotized by media. The impression it gives would have us attempting to keep up with the societal Joneses. In other words, we tend to live beyond what we can afford in order to appear important or more financially endowed. What is more important; having an extravagant event or having somewhere to live after that event? This is the sensible question I want to address in this section. As stated throughout this book, there is nothing wrong with wanting and having nice things. However, having nice things at the expense of needing to borrow money later to live is simply not wise.

For every part of your wedding, the companies and retailers you will encounter are in the business of making money. You, however, are in the business of saving and keeping as much of your hard earned money as possible. Therefore, you should be looking for bargains. Here are a few things you might want to ask yourself.

- What size and type of wedding will my budget allow me to have?

- At what location, what size reception and how many people will my budget allow me to feed?

- Does my budget allow a honeymoon trip?

- How will the wedding impact my budget timeline and the big ticket items I plan to purchase once the ceremony is over?

These are just a few of the many things to consider when planning the big day. I have seen young ladies spend extravagant amounts of money on their weddings, and be driven away in a beautiful horse-drawn carriage, only to be dropped off at a rented apartment. Unless you are Cinderella with a trust fund, you might want to reconsider a few things. Learning to be proactive instead of reactive is a key ingredient to making life happen on a budget.

If your father's name is Daddy Warbucks, an expensive wedding may not be an issue for you. Why rent, when you can own. When you rent, you are paying for another person's property and increasing the size of that person's bank account. How many of those thousands being spent could be used to make a down payment on your own home?

If you are still making car payments and your dress will cost thousands, you may be paying too much. If you have credit card debt and are paying thousands to rent space and feed others at the reception, you may be paying too much.

It is important to be realistic when making your preparations. Believe it or not, there are phenomenal ways to have a beautiful event with the appearance of expense and class without the hefty price tag. I encourage you to count the cost and the long-term effects it will have on your wallet once the event is over.

Consult with other brides. Find out what they would do differently if they had to do it all over again. Wisdom is learning from others. You will be surprised at the advice you will receive. There is a plethora of ingenious ideas out there, but you won't know until you ask.

Tip #1

"Saying Yes to the Dress"

Thinking in practical terms, how much do you really need to spend on a dress that will have limited use? When purchasing a wedding dress, most retailers will encourage you to have it preserved. This, of course, comes along with a suggestion to use one of the companies with whom they partner. The question is, for what reason are you preserving it other than the fact that you paid quite a bit of money for it? In some cases, it makes sense to preserve your investment.

I guess it all depends on the intent and purpose of ownership. There is a way around the issue. Why not rent a dress? Yes, I know every girl may have dreams of owning a wedding dress. Do you need to own the dress or own the memories you will make while wearing the dress? Your day will still be special. You will have the pictures and the memories to prove it.

However, you will not have the price tag and the leftover bills of owning it.

If you decide to purchase the dress, think of ways you can repurpose it. If you desire to own your dress, there are all sorts of crafty things you can do with it later. Redesign it and turn it into an outfit for a later occasion, perhaps an anniversary. This is just one of many ideas. Think of ways it can become part of the décor in your home. Think outside the box. The possibilities are limitless.

Tip #2

"The Venue"

The nuptial portion of the wedding ceremony lasts a good hour at best. The reception or the after-party celebration will be the largest portion of the festivities. This is where most of your special day is spent. Of course, all brides want to make this an unforgettable occasion. Since many venues charge by the hour, this is where the bride can get creative and plan accordingly.

It is amazing to see some of the ideas people come up with these days. I have watched videos of just how "out of the box" ideas couples come up when planning their weddings. Take a look at YouTube or do a Google search for creative wedding reception or banquet ideas.

Tastefully done, the banquet hall at your church or local assembly, a nearby botanical garden, or perhaps a backyard venue are all nice places to have those beautiful and memorable gatherings. Focus on putting the money where it counts the most. The money saved on the venue can be used for hiring professional caterers to serve your guests.

I have heard this referred to as "low budgeted" or "tacky." I am here to tell you; there is nothing tacky about saving money. What is tacky is not having enough money to pay your bills when the occasion is over. So, when considering the budget, think sensibly and get creative.

Tip #3

"Keeping the Honey on the Moon"

When thinking about a honeymoon trip, what comes to mind? You may be thinking of some expensive exotic Caribbean oasis or wintery resort, right? If this is not your thought, then good! A nice honeymoon does not have to be costly. Look back at the "Traveling on a Budget" tips. There are many ways to make your honeymoon dream trip a reality without breaking the bank. A major factor would be not waiting until the last minute to plan. Although you can snag some excellent last minute deals, you may not get the destination of choice.

We often overlook the beautiful places that are right in our backyard. There are many hidden gems right in the United States that are honeymoon friendly. Try searching Google for honeymoon hideaways within the United States. Those searches will then lead to other searches, and you will be surprised at what pops up.

Tip #4

"All in One"

A fabulous destination wedding would be simply marvelous. However, marvelous and fabulous come with a pretty hefty price tag or do they? It is quite possible to have your ceremony, reception, and honeymoon by way of a cruise ship. It can be an inexpensive getaway for both you and your guests. In doing so, everything you need is provided right on the ship.

Another option would be an all-inclusive getaway for you and your guests. Using the tips found in the section "traveling on a budget" look for deals. Then you be the agent and earn your free getaway by booking the trip. It might seem to be overwhelming to add something extra to a stacked to-do-list. However, considering the potential savings, this may be the incentive needed to put in the extra work. If you are a meticulous type "A" personality, you will want to hold this portion of the planning near and dear. You know what you want and how you want it. No one can relay that message better than you.

If you are planning a small wedding, the two options listed above are ideal. There would be an extra charge to reserve a private room to host your event. But, think of the time and money you would be saving by having an all-in-one event. There will be plenty of time after the wedding to enjoy many more getaways for just the two of you. For the moment and the sake of budgeting, consider the benefits of this option.

Chapter 6

Purchasing a Home on a Budget

Buying a house is something most people look forward to doing. It is considered part of the "American Dream." It is also something that should not be entered into haphazardly. In a perfect world, the ideal scenario would be to save enough money to pay cash for a home. However, we who live in the real world of the working class usually do not have the luxury of that kind of cash flow.

A loan, as defined by Merriam-Webster, is money lent to individuals at exorbitant rates of interest. Whether we would like to admit it or not, banks and lending institutions are no more than legalized loan sharks. Unfortunately, unless there is a secret entrance to a vault full of unclaimed money, we will, at some point, have to deal with these lending institutions.

Having good credit is the name of the game because having excellent credit is a game changer. Your credit and how you pay your bills says much about you. To a lender and hiring manager, it speaks to your character and integrity. Yes, now many employers require you to give them access to your credit report before they consider hiring you. Therefore, a good credit score works in your favor.

What if your credit score is less than desirable? Does that mean you will not be able to able to purchase your home? The answer is "No." It means there is some restorative work that must be done. You may think that will take years, but that is not necessarily so. There are buyer programs that can assist you on the road to recovery. Your credit may not be an issue. Good credit coupled with a buyers program puts you at an advantage. You have negotiating power and lenders will be eager for your business. Unfortunately, this was not my story.

At the young age of 27, I purchased my first home. It was a three bedroom townhouse. I was married at the time and had just given birth to my son. There were many things I did not know to do and things to look for in the small print of the mortgage agreement. It was my first time hearing about a thing called a "homeowner's association."

I had not paid much attention to the requirements and responsibilities of being a member. The number one thing is the monthly fee attached to being a member. It was a very valuable, but expensive lesson. This is one of many things to look for when purchasing property within a community of homes.

Within one year after making that purchase, I found myself separated and raising a child as a single parent. Without a second income in the household, I found myself struggling to make ends meet. Within that struggle, things happened, and the bills got behind. The impact it had on my credit was diabolical.

When you have a low credit score, most lending institutions will not touch you. If they, by some miracle, decide to take a chance, your interest rate will be on the high end. My credit score was so low the ink wasn't dry on the application before I was given the fatal "NO." It had gotten to the point that I had to "rob Peter to pay Paul." If it had just been me living alone, I would have done things quite differently, but I had someone else to look after.

Many find themselves in this same situation. My financial struggle went on for a few years, but I managed to get back on my feet. I sold the townhome and moved in with family for a few months before purchasing my next home. However, the damage to my credit remained. The good news is, I recovered well enough to get a loan, but at a higher interest rate. My credit is excellent now but at the price of many extreme but valuable lessons. The following are a few of the things I've learned along the way.

Although the process is a tedious one, I am looking forward to my next home purchase. With the knowledge I have gained, I know what to look for, and the process will be a more enjoyable experience.

Tip #1

"Credit Restoration"

The only way to true total credit restoration is to pay bills on time. This tip applies to those who find themselves with low credit scores. Here again, life happens and we all fall short at times. A key component is keeping an open line of communication with your creditors. If you know you are going to be late making a payment, call the company and make an arrangement. Do this before the account goes into default. The goal is to be proactive rather than reactive.

Negative items remain on your credit report for seven years. There are many so-called credit restoration companies. They will offer you ways to restore your credit for a fee. Remember, they are in the business to make money. What you will pay them to do, you can save your money and do the work yourself.

Once a negative balance is paid in full, companies are more willing to work with you and get that negative item removed from your credit report. This is especially true of late payment statuses. In the case of nonpayment and default items, that will require a more extensive communication effort. This may include writing letters of explanation to both the lending companies and credit reporting agencies. Make sure to inquire, as some companies may have a debt forgiveness program. This is a hidden loophole not offered unless you ask.

The desired result will not happen overnight. There is no magic wand. The process is quite time-consuming, but well worth it. The benefit of being diligent, doing the work through effective communication and honoring the debt you've made is watching your credit score increase over time.

Tip #2

"Buyer Programs"

Anyone who is thinking about purchasing a home should always invest time in search of home buyer's programs. One particular program that comes to mind is the "First-Time Home Buyer's" program. Any person who has not owned a principal residence or property within three years can qualify as a first-time home buyer according to the guidelines allocated by the FHA (Federal Housing Administration) and US Department of Housing and Urban Development. This means if this is your first home purchase, you qualify for this program. If you have not purchased a home within three years since the sale of your last home, you also qualify for this program. You can qualify to be a first time home buyer more than once. These are not the only criteria. Do your research because there may be other criteria that will cause you to be qualified.

Down-payment assistance is another program to consider. These are programs where funds are given to qualified homebuyers that can be used to cover down payment and related closing costs. The funds received through the program may be considered a grant, an interest-free loan or a debt you would have to pay off in the future. The latter I would opt out of if possible.

Each state will have its own sponsored programs designed to help first-time home buyers and others qualify for home mortgages and down payments. They are very beneficial in that they will assist you in keeping money in your pocket.

Tip #3

"You're Pre-Approved"

Being preapproved for a loan simply means a lender is ready and willing to lend you money. This is something to get excited about, especially if it is more than what you expected. Keep in mind, it is still possible for the loan to be denied even after the pre-approval process. This may be due to a number of things. One such thing would be negative items on your credit report.

Get a copy of your credit report beforehand in order to have some idea of what to expect. The amount of debt may change between the pre-approval and final approval. You will want to curb your spending habits. This is a fatal mistake made by many. A new credit report will need to be run again at the final approval process. Any new debt will show up and be taken into consideration. Most lenders require you to have employment with the same company for more than a year.

Requirements are different for each lender. These are just a few potential scenarios that could cause your loan to be denied.

There is a difference between being pre-qualified and pre-approved, which often confuses buyers. Pre-qualification is an estimation of how much you can afford to spend on your home. Pre-approval, on the other hand, means the lender has checked your credit, verified your documentation and is ready to approve a specific amount for a loan.

Buying a home is an exciting time. It is very easy to get caught up in the nostalgia of it all. Don't rush the process. Keep looking and stay within your range of affordability. Just because you have been pre-approved for an amount does not mean you **have to** purchase that amount. You will want to consider your repayment options before making this determination.

Tip #4

"Length of the Loan"

Deciding on the length of a loan is crucial. Consider the interest you will be paying in the long run before you decide. Let's calculate, for example, a low-interest rate over a period of 15-30 years. The purchase price of your home is $150,000 at an interest rate of 4.25%. At the end of 15 years, you will have paid a total of $203,115.60. At the end of 30 years, you will have paid $265,647.60.

If you are in a position to make a larger purchase and if it is in your long-range plans, by all means, go for it. Go in knowing what you are up against and count the cost.

I was shocked to learn how much of my monthly payments were paid toward the interest rather than the principal (amount of the loan). Once I learned this, I began adding extra money to my payments toward the principal balance. It helped to cut interest costs drastically. I began small and increased the amount until I began making an extra payment each month. I had to tell the bank to apply the extra payment to the principal balance only. Notice I started out slow. Not everyone will be in a position to make two payments per month. Whether it is $5 or $10, a little goes a long way when applied with wisdom. Everything you put towards paying down the principal results in a quicker payoff.

Tip #5

"Refinancing"

Not satisfied with your current interest rate? Refinancing is an option to get that rate lowered, thereby reducing your monthly payment amount. With a lower payment, you put the remaining funds into a savings account or use it pay down the principal amount as discussed in tip #4. Keep in mind this is a brand new loan. Therefore, you will have to go through a new loan process. Keep your credit in good standing so there will be a lower risk of rejection.

I first purchased my home with a 30-year mortgage agreement. After 12 years I refinanced the loan and went from a 7.25% interest rate down to a 4.25% fixed rate for a 15 year period. This saved me hundreds on my payment each month. Although my loan was for 15 years, my goal was to pay it off in 5 years. To do that it would mean paying extra on the principal. You may be asking, why not refinance for a five year period. I did not want to lock myself into the higher amount. Life happens, and I wanted to have some wiggle room just in case. With the extra, I could put money into my savings account as well as pay extra toward the principal.

Refinancing is also an option to combine some or all of your other loans. This is money smart economics. It is an excellent way to manage and save additional funds on those loans that have higher than desirable interest rates. A great idea would be to have a discussion about refinancing and consolidation options with a financial advisor.

If you are not willing to stick to a budget, this can get tricky. Refinancing does not reduce the amount you owe. It only helps you control the rate and how you repay your loan(s).

Tip #6

"Cutting Out the Middle Man"

Buying and selling real estate continues to be a big business. Once upon a time, you probably wouldn't think of buying a home without the help of an agent. That is because an agent has inside information the average Joe would not have access to without having a realtor's license. That is not the case today. Nowadays property listings, photo galleries, sales prices, history of owners, school ratings, neighborhood crime ratings and anything else you desire to know about the property is free and accessible through various real estate sites and your local government tax documents.

It will require you to do a little research to understand and obtain the necessary contracts between you and the seller. You will also need to do a little footwork to look at the different properties. Nonetheless, you would be doing this anyway with an agent. Once an agent identifies the listings, the next step would be for you go to look at the property. I don't know of any working class individuals that would spend their money sight unseen. Investing that kind of money into a property without first inspecting or having it appraised is extremely risky.

Usually, there is a 5% to 6% commission that is traditionally split between the buyer's agent and the seller's agent. Imagine what you could do with an extra few thousand dollars. Cutting out the middleman and working directly with the owners will save you money.

There are two individuals you will need to hire. One is an inspector. A property inspector is necessary to let you know what, if anything, is going on with the property before you buy. You will want to have this information to avoid any unnecessary expense of having to fix things you were not made aware of before the purchase. You can then use this information to negotiate and deduct any necessary repairs from the asking price. Make sure to hire an inspector with an excellent reputation who is known for doing a thorough job.

In addition to hiring someone to inspect the property, you will have to hire a real estate attorney. This is the one who will handle all of the legal documents on the day of closing. Be prepared to sign your life away, because that is what it will probably feel like. Just kidding, but really, you will be signing your name quite a few times on that day.

Since you already have to pay an attorney take advantage of his/her expert knowledge. Ask questions about the property. The attorney will be able to provide you with the same information as the agent. If he/she does not have the answer, expect guidance on how and where to look.

Chapter 7

Car Purchase on a Budget

Purchasing a vehicle is also considered a major purchase. After your mortgage, a car payment is likely to be the next-biggest item in your monthly budget. This is especially true for those of us within the working class. As much as we would love not having those monthly deductions, a vehicle is one item we will find ourselves having to purchase more than once over the course of a lifetime. Enjoy those in between times, save and budget accordingly.

There is no magical formula. The same principles apply here as they do with purchasing a home. A few things to consider are the retail price, the cost and amount of upkeep the vehicle will require. This is a budgeting concern. The type of car you purchase will determine the cost of maintenance. For example, the cost of an oil change will be significantly different in a Mercedes, BMW, or a Lexus than it would be for a Toyota, Honda or Hyundai. Over the course of 5-10 years, the amount of maintenance, insurance, cost of gas, and potential repairs will be something to add to your budgeting equation. Each vehicle purchase will enable you to budget more wisely and better understand the cost of owning a vehicle.

I typically hold onto my vehicles for as long as I possibly can. Let me give you an idea of how long I tend to keep my vehicles. In 1997, when purchasing my next vehicle, I attempted to use the vehicle I already owned as a trade-in. It was about 15 years old and had been patched up so many times that the salesman offered me $400 to keep it.

My desire had always been to purchase new instead of used. Until 2008, my budget did not allow it. Although I could afford to make the purchase, the dread of having a car payment was a huge deterrent. I held off for as long as I could. After much research and a few additional mechanical breakdowns, November 2010 was when my dream of owning a new car became a reality.

Tip #1

"Never Commit to the First Offer"

The primary goal of a car salesperson is to convince you to spend more money than you originally planned. They'll try to entice you by any means necessary. This is another purchase area where competition can work in your favor. Car dealerships will compete to win your business.

The car purchasing process can become frustrating. Never commit to anything before you have an opportunity to visit at least 2 or 3 dealerships. Once you find the one you want, learn the invoice price versus the (MSRP) manufacturer's suggested retail price. The invoice price is the amount the dealership paid. Compare this to the price for which they are selling the vehicle. This will give you an idea of the dealership markup.

Given the incredible variations between invoice and retail cost of what the dealership is asking for, you will also want to check the Kelly Blue Book price. "The Kelly Blue Book" is a nationally recognized report of the value prices for both new and used vehicles based on actual transactions of what others are paying. These amounts are adjusted regularly as market conditions change. Knowing what you are working with allows you to negotiate a better purchase price.

The profit margin on many vehicles, especially newer models, normally depends on the demand. If the vehicle is in high demand, the dealership knows selling them will not be a problem. Because of this, they may not be as eager to negotiate with you. However, it never hurts to try. Most salespeople work on commission and are eager to make a sale.

Once you have gotten the dealership to commit to selling at a certain price, don't stop there. Ask for a copy of the purchase agreement. With this in hand, you can use it to shop around and negotiate for a better price at another dealership. Once other dealerships get a look at their competitors' offer, they may be willing to offer you a better deal or more options for the same amount. Take your research to the internet and make a price comparison. Print this out as well and use it as another bargaining tool.

Tip #2

"Go In Ready"

Don't assume financing at the dealership is the best deal. When the dealership arranges financing options, they are simply doing something you can do better on your own. They are simply forwarding your information to one or more prospective auto lenders. If the lender chooses to finance your loan, they may authorize or quote an interest rate to the dealer to finance your loan. The interest rate you negotiate with the dealer may be higher than the one you obtain on your own because it most likely will include an amount that compensates the dealer for handling the financing.

By getting preapproved or securing your loan beforehand, you go in ready. It is the same as having cash. The salesman does not have to know it's a loan. They only need to see your ability to purchase a car. This is an additional layer of negotiating power.

Tip #3

"Nearly New"

Have you heard it said, "The moment a car leaves the lot, it loses its value?" What dealerships fail to tell you is that your shiny new vehicle will depreciate at least 10-12% the moment you drive it off the lot. After five years, it'll only be worth approximately 40% of what you paid for it.

Every car that I purchased before 2010 was a used vehicle. Of course, used cars are always less expensive than new ones. Buying what I call "nearly new" means purchasing a used car within the same model year. I discovered that many of the rental car agencies will upgrade their vehicles every year and sell their previous models to local dealers. This was how I ended up with my new, yet used vehicle. Because it was still within the model year, it remained under the manufacturers' warranty.

Tip #4

"Know the Facts"

Before making any large purchase, I encourage you, ALWAYS do your research. This is especially true if you are purchasing a used vehicle. One of the most important things when purchasing a used vehicle is to obtain a CARFAX report. Unfortunately, there are quite a few shady dealerships out there. This report will provide safeguards and prevent you from purchasing a lemon. It provides you with a history of the vehicle and includes information such as:

- Vehicle Registration
- Structural Damage
- Accident History
- Odometer Reading
- Service & Repair Information
- Lemon History
- Usage (taxi, rental, lease, etc.)

Most dealerships will provide you a CARFAX report upon asking. If not, you can always obtain one online. Make sure the VIN on the report matches the VIN on the vehicle you are purchasing. The VIN is the abbreviation for "Vehicle Identification Number" which is a personalized ID card for every vehicle.

You will also want to compare the price of the vehicle by using the Kelly Blue Book. It will give you a general idea of fair market pricing and help you avoid paying too much.

Chapter 8

Furnishing on a Budget

The blissful ignorance of youth is not having the responsibilities of adulthood. Paying bills is one thing, but it would be nice if the furnishings were included. In the pilot episode of the Cosby show, Bill teaches his son, Theo, one of life's very important lessons about living on a budget. He teaches him the limitations of wanting, but not being able to have everything he wants, but can't afford.

I furnished my first apartment with items from local discount furniture stores. The furniture served its purpose for a time. I took care of it, so it lasted for as long as I needed it. As my income increased, I could then afford to purchase more sturdy items. Of course, that was more expensive as well. I am not an impulse buyer. Life has taught me to be a bargain shopper. I tend to research and weigh my options, especially when it comes to spending a significant amount of money. Anything that costs more than a few hundred dollars classifies as a significant purchase. Appliances and furniture may not be considered major purchases, but they do fall under the budget line item of "significant purchases" category.

Appliances and furniture are items that represent your lifestyle. They speak to your unique design and style. This is another area of purchase where you want to take your time and count the cost. Consider your choices wisely because these are big ticket items that will be with you for some time.

How many times have you purchased something only to experience regret later for not getting the one with more or better features? If you are not satisfied, you may be able to return it for an upgrade, especially if you are getting the more expensive one. This is, of course, as long as it is within the 30, 60, or 90 day grace period. Unfortunately, we only realize we want the better one long after we've had the items for a while. It happens to all of us at one time or another.

Research the items and find out what options are available, what model, and if there is a newer version or style about to be released. This is especially true when it comes to appliances. I have included a couple of tips I used when making such purchases.

I encourage you to spend some time shopping around. Do your homework and make sure to compare prices. It can be an adrenalin rush to save money. So, have fun making your interior preparations and decorations happen on a budget.

Tip #1

"Scratch & Dent"

You might want to visit the scratch and dent section before you purchase any furniture and appliances. Some retailers will sell you these at a highly discounted rate rather than send them back to the manufacturer and make nothing. For instance, a recently purchased bedroom dresser with an original price tag of $900 was sold for $150. The only defect was a small indentation at the bottom. It was not visible and if you can live with it, look at the savings. In many cases, the damage may be repairable for little to no extra cost. It may only require a little ingenuity on your part. For those appliances that will probably be tucked away in a laundry room somewhere, this is a steal of a deal.

If that particular store does not have a "scratch & dent" section, call around. All stores will not sell defective items, but many do.

Tip #2

"Slightly Damaged or Irregular"

Other than scratch and dent, some stores might have a section within their inventory that is considered "damaged" or "slightly damaged," with "slightly" being the operative word. The damage could be something simple and easily repairable such as an upholstery tear, a minor discoloration in the fabric, a dented leg or chipped paint, or broken handle, etc.

The last set of chairs I purchased had one of these slightly damaged issues. I purchased a leather chair set. Where the cow was branded, it showed up on the ottoman. The branding iron appeared to be the shape of a horseshoe or the letter U. For that reason, the furniture company decided to discount the piece in my favor. That was a win for me. Besides, I thought the imperfection gave the piece character and showed the authenticity of the leather. As the old saying goes, "it's all in the eye of the beholder."

Do not discount your local discount furniture stores. You can find some hidden gems in those as well. More and more of the discount retailers are now selling what appears to be quality furniture. This is because these items are considered "irregular." The term "irregular" simply means the items are slightly-imperfect and did not meet the manufacturer's quality guidelines. The discount store purchases them, and the savings are then passed along to the bargain shoppers.

Tip #3

"Buy Used"

Buying used furniture and appliances does not necessarily mean second-hand as you may find in a thrift shop or yard sale. I encourage you not to exclude thrift shops and yard sales. You will be surprised at what you might find. How many times have you heard or read about someone making a 2 or 3 dollar purchase from their local goodwill or thrift shop only to find out later the item was worth thousands of dollars. Steals, deals and quality items are often overlooked.

The type of used furniture I am referring to in this tip is customer rejection. This is when customers change their minds about the purchase and for whatever reason, return the items to the store. Once this happens, many retailers will no longer sell the items as new. They are then considered used items. It may even be possible to negotiate for extreme discounts.

If you are one that does not mind purchasing items from the showroom floor, this is another excellent way to save. Many retailers will not sell their showroom stock. For the ones that do, they are also considered used. I am a little particular, however, about the types of items I purchase from the showroom floor. Some things are simply off limits, such as a set of mattresses. Even though they may not have been slept on per se, they have been tried on for size by many. If this is not a problem for you, it could be a bargain for you.

Tip #4

"Online Purchases"

Many shoppers are hands-on buyers. I am one of those buyers who has to visualize, touch and feel an item before making the purchase. I am one who has to visualize how furniture is going to fit in a particular area of my home before I commit to buying. Because of this need, many of us tend to stay away from purchasing furniture over the internet. Don't be alarmed. I have discovered a remedy.

There are excellent deals to be had by shopping online. You can compare prices right at your fingertips if you know what you want to purchase. Use your local merchants to do your window shopping. Once you have decided on what you would like to buy, then you are ready to make your online purchases. You might be surprised at the number of merchants who have what you need and the different variations. Now that you have an idea, you are ready to do your online search. When you locate your items, contact the merchant and try using some of the negotiating tips I've shared with you.

You will want to obtain product name, number and any other pertinent information needed to make sure the products match. Compare product information and prices as each vendor the manufacturer is using to purchase their inventory from may be different. In this case, it is always a good idea to inquire about the return policy as an extra precaution. You may need to return your items if they are not as described. Many retailers have free shipping, but you will want to double check and not get charged for being unaware.

Chapter 9

Teaching Children to Budget

When you see a little girl with her stand on the corner, buy ALL the lemonade. When the neighborhood kids come by asking to sweep, mow or rake your yard, even if it is not needed, let them do something. Then make sure to **pay** them. Whenever and however you can, we need to encourage the drive, initiative, and the entrepreneurial spirit in our children. We will then watch them grow to be responsible adults.

As my mother taught me, I decided I should do likewise in teaching my son the value of hard work and spending his money wisely. I started him a business when he was ten years old. It was called

"Elijah's Chore Service." I purchased him a cleaning caddy with a few supplies. We printed a set of business cards and made it all official. This set the groundwork and gave him a sense of ownership.

On the weekend I would take him over to a couple of **trustworthy** elders and allow him to do little chores around their house. This was helpful for both of them. He could do things they could no longer do or had trouble doing. It was a way for the elders to have a little company. It was a way of teaching him the responsibility of working.

I did not set a price for his services. The experience was not about money. It was more about teaching him the value of working for what you want. It introduced him to the reality that we do not always get what we want.

I would buy the things he needed. When it came to things he wanted, I encouraged him to use the money he earned. This caused him to think and evaluate need versus want, nurturing his ability to prioritize and make wise decisions. The lessons he learned from this experience are still paying off. One important lesson was learning how to save money.

When he turned thirteen, he wanted to do more and decided to branch out into lawn care. He made a set of flyers and acquired a few clients doing light yard work on the weekends. He is now 27 years old and still maintains his lawn care business. It is now called "Lawn Barbers."

The business has grown so much that he now employs his younger cousins. He has grown into quite the responsible adult. He lives on his own, works a full-time 9-5, and is in the process of completing a master's degree. Every now and again I will ask if he needs my help with anything because it tickles me and does my heart good to hear him say "No ma'am, I'm straight."

For the past 15 years, I have worked in the human services, training & development field. I have witnessed the domino effect and pitfalls of entitlement thinking. Many misguided people believe the world owes them something. That is having an entitlement syndrome. People who think that way become angry when they do not get what they want. If adults do not model and teach children a better way, they will not know or grow to maximize their potential. Let's continue to encourage them even if they are not born to us.

Tip #1

"The Co-Worker's Role"

Parents sometimes tend to take on their children's projects as their own. Let them be the driving force behind their idea(s). Help develop them with your excitement and support. If you think the project is too much for them to handle, gently guide them in another direction. Your enthusiasm for their ideas will encourage them to continue. Keep in mind that you will have to devote much of your time keeping them on track and making things happen for them.

They will probably lose interest at some point due to their immature attention span. You will then have teachable moments for lessons in dependability and endurance. Ask them often what they need you to do as their co-worker or employee. This becomes an opportunity to teach them leadership skills and how to be a good manager. You are shaping your child's future. Everything you do through this project will yield great rewards. Not only will you teach them discipline, they will also experience lessons in management while learning how to run a business. This may start out as "play" but will quickly turn into opportunities for learning valuable life lessons.

Tip #2

"A Silent Partnership"

We tend to appreciate things more when we work for them rather than when they are given to us. I believe this is because of the energy and drive we put into the work it takes to own it. In doing so, it helps them avoid the snares of the entitlement syndrome.

Allow your child(ren) to spend the money they earn to purchase the equipment and supplies they need for their business. The business will then become more personal, and they will appreciate the hard work and investment. Of course, you can and will want to assist them, but they do not have to know how much you have contributed. Allow them to be the majority partner and allow yourself to function as the silent partner. When you feel the need to help, look for subtle ways to put money back into their business.

Tip #3

"Dollar for Dollar"

Teaching children how to invest in their financial future can never begin too soon. Imagine what a retirement fund would look like even at the age of 25 if started ten years prior. With the proper guidance, a child is never too young to invest and become self-made million and billionaires.

The hands-on technique is a great motivator. As much as possible, allow your children to accompany you to the bank and speak with representatives about investing money. Encourage them to participate and ask questions. As an incentive, match the money they earn such as employers do with 401K plans. Use this opportunity to teach them the principles of borrowing money. Find a low-risk stock and allow them to invest in the stock market. Online banking is not just for adults. Children are very computer savvy. With your guidance, they will be able to monitor their accounts and watch their investments grow.

Sample Budget Sheet

Expenditure	Total Due	Amount Paid
Rent	$	
Lights	$	
Water	$	
Gas	$	
Phone	$	
Internet	$	
Food	$	
	$	
	$	
	$	

Miscellaneous Expenditures

	$	
	$	
	$	

Monthly Total: _____
Monthly Income: _____
$ _____

Here is a simple budget sheet that can be used to get an idea of monthly spending needs and habits. Subtract monthly income from monthly totals. Divide the rest and stick to your budget plan. Emergencies do happen. Therefore, it may be a good idea to add a "rainy day" line item. Any money left over is to be split between the miscellaneous items such as savings, travel/vacation funds, etc.

If your monthly salary is less than your monthly bills, some serious adjustments need to happen. This means you are living beyond your means. Try this for at least two months to give yourself an idea of how and where you are spending your money. It might surprise you.

Some of the hard questions we all have to ask ourselves are:

- Do I really need all the things I am spending my money on?
- Do I really need these things right now?
- What can and cannot wait?

If we sit for a moment and take inventory of our spending habits, I believe a reality check will be a huge money saver.

Chapter 10

At the End of the Day

For where your treasure is, there will your heart be also (Matthew 6:21)

The ideal order of things would be to grow up, get a good education, obtain an award-winning career with a six-figure salary and live on easy street for the rest of our lives. Let's be real. How often does that happen? The reality is that many of us find ourselves among those who are not working because we want to; we work because we need proper income to survive.

Life happens, and when it does, we often find ourselves having to cope with undesirable conditions. But what does not kill us only makes us stronger. We do what we can with what we have and by doing so, we make life happen.

Poverty and lack are not only physical conditions, they are also mental conditions. Whatever a person believes, that person becomes. What we choose to focus on will become our reality. We will make the necessary steps to becoming the way we see ourselves even before it materializes. To do that, we must establish priorities and govern ourselves accordingly.

At the end of the day, budgeting is about prioritizing. If your heart is into what you are doing, whatever you are doing will receive adequate time and attention. It requires discipline, but it will be well worth the effort, and the payoff is rewarding.

"Champagne taste on a root beer salary" means having expensive desires and spending money without the means to obtain and maintain the lifestyle. I have witnessed this on many occasions. Enjoying life doesn't have to be expensive. As members of the working class, we simply need to be honest and realistic when it comes to money matters. More should not be going out than the amount coming in.

There is absolutely nothing wrong with owning nice things. However, we must consider the reality of our situational budget. If owning nice things results in experiencing lack, wisdom is not being applied. Do what you can until you are able to do more, or what you consider to be better.

Other areas in our lives require budgeting consideration. These are a few instances and occasions where I have experienced the benefit of saving money, which is always a plus. Had I known then what I know now, I would have done things quite differently. I would have used wisdom and made better decisions about how I spent my money.

I cannot stress enough the importance of budget counseling when you are deciding to make major purchases. There is a saying that "what you don't know can't hurt you." However, I disagree. I believe what you don't know can and will cost you time and quite a bit of money. I hope these tips will be of good use in helping you save money.

Like so many of the working class, I have experienced the struggles of making ends meet. It was not pleasant being a single parent, but it taught me many valuable lessons. Hopefully, by sharing my experiences, they will help you keep more of your hard-earned money in your pocket.

Saving money is not a requirement, but it is often necessary. My goal in providing you with these simple tips and tools is to encourage you to save. As mentioned previously, I know all too well the pains of trying to make ends meet. For many of the working-class, this is a real struggle. The decisions we make today can either make or break us tomorrow.

Life is meant to be enjoyed, but, it doesn't require spending large amounts of money to make that happen. Go on vacation, travel the world, shop and buy things that make you happy. Just use wisdom while doing it. You will thank yourself later.

**Your money matters!
Make it count.**

About the Author

Passionately driven are words that describe Veronica. Believing that whatever you do, you should be a specialist at it; she holds a Bachelor of Arts degree in Public Administration from Shaw University and a Master of Education degree in Training & Development from North Carolina State University She often states that training is a part of her DNA and believes everyone is born with a purpose. Unfortunately, many never realize that purpose. Therefore, she is a motivator who encourages individuals to pursue their dreams until those dreams become a reality.

On occasion, it takes another person to help us see what we may not see in ourselves. Veronica is known for her ability to ignite enthusiasm while motivating others who simply need direction, insight or that extra push toward accomplishing their goals. Such keen insight allows her to empower both young and old to uncover hidden talent, discover additional abilities and develop areas of untapped potential within themselves.

In her role as a Trainer, Motivational Speaker, Life Coach and Ordained Minister, she is known for her tenacious "Making Life Happen" leadership style. Her unique approach to training has been instrumental in assisting both individuals and groups in the areas of personal, professional and leadership growth and development. She is a multifaceted trainer who empowers others to "think outside the box."

Available for conferences, workshops, seminars, motivation and training events upon request.

For more information and to request scheduling for your next event, please visit:

www.veronicatrains.com

Other Resources Materials

The search for satisfaction and fulfillment is a part of being human. It is a cry of the heart and an innate longing we all have. When life happens and it will, we often search for something greater outside of ourselves. This search causes us to look for something more than what we already know or have experienced. That something is the presence of God and the sweet communion of His Holy Spirit.

Every loving relationship has to be cultivated and nurtured. Developing a relationship with God is not exempt from this process. To know Him, we must make spending time with Him a priority. Our knowledge and love for God is developed through our pursuit of Him. Understanding the power of His love causes us to walk in greater levels of victory. This is a testament to life and freedom through intimate pursuit. It is a glimpse into one daughter's journey to know the Father.

Veronica's experiences of getting to know God as Father in her book entitled "In the Garden of His Presence" coupled with this devotional journal is designed to inspire and encourage you along your journey into deeper levels of intimacy with the Holy Spirit. You will discover that the answers to everything we need can be found in the Garden of His Presence.

There is a purpose for your life. Your journey is personal and specifically designed with a distinct plan from heaven. There is so much more you have yet to discover. It is always good to know about God, but how much more beneficial would it be to experience Him? His thoughts about you are good and very intentional. Therefore, your time with Him must also be intentional. Precious treasures are waiting to be discovered that are hidden in Father's heart. During your intimate times of fellowship, you will be awakened to His desires and plan for your life.

Awaiting you in this 31-day devotional prayer journal are articles of encouragement and prayers of agreement for life and situations we all face. Veronica co-authors this journal with you as she shares some of her experiences and lessons learned along the way. If journaling is something new to you, this is an excellent resource to help you begin. If you journal regularly, this is an additional tool designed to encourage you on your journey.

The answers to everything you need can be found in the Garden of His Presence.

But Jesus called them unto him, and said, Suffer little children to come unto me, and forbid them not: for of such is the kingdom of God. Luke 18:16

Introduce your child to a relationship with Jesus Christ. Proverbs 22:6 teaches us to "Train up a child in the way they should go, and when they are old, they will not depart from it."

Read along with your child(ren) as they learn about our Heavenly Father. This book will introduce them to Jesus and help them understand that He is always with them everywhere they go.

Copyright © 2018 – by Veronica G. Burnette
All Rights Reserved

www.ingramcontent.com/pod-product-compliance
Lightning Source LLC
Chambersburg PA
CBHW060803050426
42449CB00008B/1506